The Taxman Alw

BDO Stoy Hayward LLP is the UK member firm of BDO International, the world's fifth largest accountancy network, with more than 600 offices in 100 countries. We specialise in helping businesses, whether start-ups or multinationals, to grow. Through our own professional expertise and by working directly with organisations, we've developed a robust understanding of the factors that govern business growth. Our objective is to help our clients maximise their potential.

Daniel Dover is a partner in BDO Stoy Hayward, where he specialises in HMRC investigations. His expertise covers all United Kingdom HMRC Specialist Investigations office matters, including those involving questions of domicile and residence of both corporate and private entities. Daniel also advises a wide range of charities on the tax pitfalls they face. He inspired and created *Daddy Fool*, *Charitable Trysts* and *Russian Roulette*, three short film dramatisations depicting people falling foul of HMRC, all of which can be seen on YouTube and on the BDO website at www.bdo.co.uk/taxinvestigations.

Tim Hindle is the author of several books on finance and business and was the founder director of *Eurobusiness*. He has been editor of *Director* magazine and management and finance editor of *The Economist*.

Daniel and Tim previously co-authored *An Inspector Calls*, *An Inspector Returns* and *War or Peace*, all on the subject of HMRC investigations and published by Profile.

The Taxman Always Rings Twice

What to do when the Revenue pays a call

Daniel Dover
and
Tim Hindle

with cartoons by
McLachlan

PROFILE BOOKS

First published in Great Britain in 2009 by
PROFILE BOOKS LTD
3A Exmouth House
Pine Street
Exmouth Market
London ECIR OJH
www.profilebooks.com

A CIP catalogue record for this book is available from the British Library.

ISBN 978 1 84668 280 3

Typeset in Columbus by MacGuru Ltd
info@macguru.org.uk
Printed in the UK by CPI Bookmarque, Croydon, CRO 4TD

While care has been taken to ensure the accuracy of the contents of this
book, it is intended to provide general guidance only and does not
constitute professional advice. The information contained in this book is
based on the authors' understanding of legislation, regulation and practice at
the time of publication, all of which is subject to change, possibly with
retrospective effect. Neither they nor BDO Stoy Hayward LLP can therefore
accept any legal or regulatory liability from readers acting on the
information given.

Mixed Sources
Product group from well-managed
forests and other controlled sources
www.fsc.org Cert no. TT-COC-002227
© 1996 Forest Stewardship Council

Contents

Acknowledgements

We are most grateful to many people for their help in the production of this book.

To Stuart Gerber at BDO Stoy Hayward LLP and Andrew Franklin and Paul Forty at Profile who have helped, encouraged and cajoled throughout its production.

To Fiona Fernie, Frank Goldberg, John Hood and Dawn Register for their expert knowledge so patiently revealed; and to Sarah Rix for making it happen. Outside BDO Stoy Hayward LLP, thanks are due to our wives Helen and Ellian, who have provided us with constant support throughout our careers and have endured the many unsocial hours we have spent in working to deadlines or assisting clients in trouble.

Last, a word of thanks to the main protagonists of the tax investigation: Her Majesty's Revenue & Customs, without whom …

Daniel Dover
Tim Hindle
June 2009

Foreword

No one likes paying tax.

Most people worry at some time or another about their tax returns and about keeping their financial affairs in order. But it can, and sometimes does, get worse. If the investigator from Her Majesty's Revenue & Customs (HMRC) is on your tail it can be both disruptive and distressing.

When the taxman rings the doorbell, any one of a number of emotions is common. Reactions vary from denial that the matter might be serious, anger with the 'unjustness' of it all – or just sheer terror at the thought of losing everything and ending up in prison. But all is not lost. The advice from any experienced professional is: don't panic, and get expert help at the outset – *before* the taxman has a chance to ring twice. You will need someone on your side who knows the jargon and understands how HMRC operates.

If you are subjected to HMRC scrutiny, this book, which combines and updates our previous books, *An*

Inspector Returns and *War or Peace,* will give you a clearer idea of what lies ahead and how best to get through it. However, whatever you do, don't skirmish seriously with HMRC without decent intelligence – far more is needed than is provided in this slim volume.

Good luck – and get help.

THE
TAXMAN
ALWAYS
RINGS TWICE

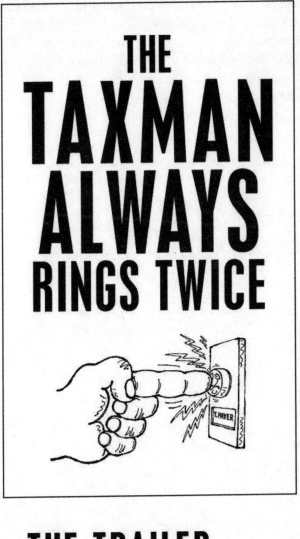

THE TRAILER . . .

Introduction

Consider this book to be like a trailer for a movie, a movie called *The Taxman Always Rings Twice*, or *Taxman* for short. The movie tells the story of an enquiry into your personal tax affairs by Her Majesty's Revenue & Customs (HMRC) – a hybrid organisation formed by the merger of the Inland Revenue with the Customs & Excise in 2005.

Many of the elements essential to great movies are to be found in *Taxman*. For example:

- **There is something important at stake.**
  In *Indiana Jones and the Raiders of the Lost Ark*, the important thing was nothing less than the Ark of the Covenant and the saving of mankind. Here it is not quite so dramatic. But the audience for *Taxman* will be glued to their seats waiting to see whether you, the taxpayer, go to jail or not.
- **There are obstacles in the way.**
  In detective stories there are those moments when

the audience wonders if the witness can be persuaded to go into the stand and testify. In *Taxman* there are nail-biting moments while the taxpayer waits to hear whether his former spouse has mentioned their second home in Marbella or the deposits in some far offshore tax haven. And there are times when the viewer wonders whether the taxpayer's mother will admit that her suitcase was not full of gnomes when she returned from a day trip to Geneva.

- **There is a hook to grab the public's attention.** In most movies this is a big-name star or an exotic location. *Taxman* is stronger on the latter than the former. Many of the world's leading offshore centres happen to be housed on small, beautiful islands – Jersey, Bermuda, the Cayman Islands, and so on. On the other hand, while the real-life stars of this story are likely to be rich, and they may once have been briefly famous, they are not going to look like Kristin Scott Thomas or Daniel Craig.
- **There are great heroes and great villains.** The audience may start by assuming that the taxpayer is the hero and the tax investigator* the villain. But this type of story may well turn out the other way. After all, it was plain vanilla taxmen who finally nailed Al Capone. And an increasingly

---

*Investigators in HMRC are no longer referred to as inspectors. 'Inspector' is therefore used in this book only when referring to a time when the term was in general use, or in a direct quotation.

popular plot these days is the one where a criminal is jailed not for his drug-dealing or financial scams but for the tax that he never paid. So be prepared to feel warmly towards the taxman in the movie.

Rumour has it that Colin Firth was keen on the role.

As for its genre, *Taxman* is a tense thriller with the ever-present possibility of a disturbing ending. It is definitely not a comfortable romance where the audience knows in advance that everybody will live happily ever after.

The movie may well cause stress and anxiety for some viewers, and most people will not want to experience it on their own. Be sure to have someone with you, someone who knows from experience how such stories tend to unfold, and who understands the taxman's jargon – for there is plenty of that. To an inexperienced ear, the plot can sound as incomprehensible as the first 30 minutes of *Quantum of Solace*, the 2008 all-action James Bond movie.

The audience is encouraged to sympathise with the taxman because it is made clear that he (or she) is right in the middle of an identity crisis. In the old days, tax inspectors wrote polite letters from musty offices after they had finished the *Times* crossword; nowadays, investigators are more likely to knock on doors (many times and in rapid succession) on their way back from a martial arts class. Investigations into people's failure to pay tax these

days roll out more like a Guy Ritchie movie than something from the pen of Richard Curtis, creator of *Notting Hill* and *Four Weddings and a Funeral*.

This little book aims to give a flavour of the full film. It looks at the cast of characters in the movie, including you, the taxpayer; your professional adviser; and the taxman. It takes a glance at some of the locations used. These range across the globe, from no-expenses-spared Caribbean hideaways to the inside of Wormwood Scrubs. And it also looks at some of the props involved (repossessed super-yachts and bags of cash, for example).

The book goes on to provide an invaluable guide to some of the jargon used in tax investigations before it gives a summary of the movie's screenplay and then quotes some of the lines that give key clues to the rapidly unfolding plot.

HEALTH WARNING

Reading this book is a lot more fun than having to sit through the movie...

Dramatis personae (the cast)

You, the taxpayer (or not, as the case may be)

Taxpayers come in all shapes and sizes. Some are petrified by the prospect of any sort of tussle with the taxman; others become unbelievably belligerent and aggressive well before any sort of wrongdoing has been established. As one investigator puts it in the movie: 'There will always be folks prepared to argue with a lamp-post if no more stimulating option is available.'

Whatever your shape, size or temperament, you, the taxpayer, are the star of this show and are likely to appear in most of the scenes. So it is important for you to stay fit. You should take regular physical exercise and, if you do fall ill, get a doctor's certificate to that effect. HMRC is not unsympathetic to ill health. A taxpayer who is elderly and frail will not be subjected to interrogation. But that does not mean there will be no investigation of their affairs.

As a society we are ageing, and more and more wealth is accumulating in the hands of the elderly. This means that an increasing number of those who come under investigation may be ill-equipped to cope with it. There is another group, the 'burnt out but opulent' (or BOBOs), that is equipped to cope but simply doesn't have the time. Technology has increased the pace of BOBOs' lives dramatically in recent years and they are hard pressed to find either the time or the energy demanded by a full investigation.

Successful entrepreneurs are also ill-equipped to cope with a full investigation. Businessmen with enough income and/or assets to catch HMRC's eye tend to be people who are in control of their lives. They are accustomed to getting what they want and have spent much of their working lives trying to find ways round obstacles. Normally they score points for succeeding, and for doing so better than anyone else. A letter from a taxman saying that they are under investigation undermines their sense of being in control.

Then there is the shame and embarrassment of it. The fact that you are under investigation by HMRC is not a subject for everyday dinner-party conversations. Everyone has skeletons they'd rather keep hidden in their cupboards. Once you are caught up in an investigation, however, you realise that you might have to expose yourself and your innermost thoughts. Not only to a professional adviser, but also to a government agency.

The non-dom

The non-domiciled or 'non-dom' is a variety of taxpayer that is more talked about than seen. It includes Russian billionaires and Arab sheikhs living not a muezzin's call away from Marble Arch. Non-doms are people who live in the United Kingdom (UK) but were not born here, and who declare that they do not intend to die here. (There are a few cases where the children of non-domiciled parents have established non-domiciled status for themselves even though they were born in the UK and spent much of their lives in this country.) Non-doms are subject to a different tax regime from ordinary UK taxpayers, one that is much less onerous.

The treatment they receive differs according to the tax. As far as inheritance tax is concerned, people become 'deemed domiciled' in the UK once they have been resident here for 17 out of the past 20 years. But for the purposes of income tax and capital-gains tax they can remain non-domiciled for the whole of their lives, unless they married a UK-domiciled person before 1974.

Residence is a different concept, but also important for tax purposes. Someone's residence is determined by the number of days that they spend in the country. In general, if they spend fewer than 90 nights in the UK in each year they are deemed to be non-resident. But there are special rules for people like airline pilots and cabin crew who spend much of their time working in the air, resident (in effect) in no man's land.

In this day and age, when passports are rarely stamped for travellers going from one European Union (EU) country to another, it is not as easy for HMRC to demonstrate that taxpayers have failed to observe the non-residence rules. One non-resident claims always to return to the UK on the Eurostar train from Paris (inside it, not underneath it) on the grounds that passports are never stamped on that particular cross-Channel trip (possibly not realising that the names are recorded by Eurostar).

The names of all passengers passing through airports, however, are preserved for years. And credit-card and telephone bills invariably tell a story of their own. People like sailors, who spend long spells abroad, like to carry large amounts of cash when returning home on leave. That way they do not need to use credit cards, which leave a trail of the time they spend in the UK.

Until recently, the income that non-doms received overseas was taxed in the UK only to the extent that it was remitted to this country. However, beginning with the 2008/09 tax year, non-doms can opt for this so-called 'remittance basis' of taxation only if they pay £30,000 a year to HMRC. For many, this is still less onerous than it would be in other countries, and it is the basis of continuing claims that the UK is a tax haven for the super-rich. In the United States, all residents (and, indeed, all passport holders) are taxed on their worldwide income and capital gains regardless of where it arises and of where they want to be buried.

Non-doms behave differently from other UK residents. In the first place, their status encourages them to do as much shopping as possible outside the UK. So they make frequent trips to Paris and New York. That way they can pay for goods with money that stays legitimately outside the UK tax net.

So not only do they avoid paying direct taxes into Britain's coffers, they also avoid paying UK indirect taxes like Value Added Tax (VAT). *Taxman* views them as a strange anomaly that governments would love to get rid of, but do not yet dare to.

Professional advisers

Professional advisers do not have a cameo role in this movie: they feature prominently. They are a bit like the counsel for the defence in the classic courtroom drama.

Getting professional advice is one sure way to reduce the pain of an investigation – both the financial and the emotional pain. Advisers can initially appear expensive, but at the end of the day they may save you from prison or, at least, sharply reduce your tax bill. Those who have been in the business for a while swear that had

they been working on a contingency basis – earning a percentage of the tax that they legitimately save their clients – they would today be very rich indeed.

One big advantage of having an adviser is the on-going communication that he or she has established with HMRC. Advisers spend their lives dealing with tax investigators. If anyone understands those strange creatures, they do. An adviser can phone an investigator if a deadline is approaching, and fend off the risk of a heavy-handed reminder. It is a very rare taxpayer who will feel sufficiently relaxed about his tax affairs to ring HMRC to tell them that he's going to be late sending in the forms that have been requested.

As far as HMRC is concerned, a taxpayer can choose to be professionally represented at any stage in the proceedings, and can change advisers in mid-stream. HMRC will deal with whoever is put before them.

Advisers often end up becoming the confidant of their clients, because in this type of movie there are not many people that taxpayers can trust – especially when they have lots of trusts (see page 67). The more trusts, the less trust.

Much of what is disclosed to an adviser is covered by the law on privilege, but not all of it. Any communication intended to facilitate a crime, for example, is very definitely excluded. It is best to clarify with your adviser from the very beginning what is and is not covered by the law on privilege, because it does change from time to time.

The tax investigator

Making movies that focus on the lives of tax investigators is not as far-fetched as it might at first seem. *The Tax Inspector* is the title of a novel by the Australian Booker-prize-winning author Peter Carey. How many other professions have achieved such elevation? *The Part-Time Plumber* has yet to be written, as has *The Hedge-Fund Manager*. What's more, Carey's tax inspector is a woman. And she's pregnant and unmarried.

A tax inspector's job description

The work is intellectually stimulating, with early responsibility. Tax inspectors investigate the accuracy of tax returns and accounts submitted to HMRC. Typical work activities include:

- applying tax legislation to companies, partnerships, organisations and individuals;
- examining accounts and researching background material;
- investigating fraud;
- giving expert advice on taxation matters to companies, partnerships, organisations and individuals;
- negotiating tax settlements with taxpayers and/or accountants;
- representing HMRC at independent appeal tribunals in disputed cases.

In those cases which result in a full enquiry being carried out, typical work activities are likely to include:

- looking into the finances of a business to find out exactly how it operates;
- examining the records kept and taking into account the lifestyle of the proprietor or directors;

- visiting business premises and meeting people face to face during the investigation;
- reviewing in detail aspects of the business accounts to ensure that tax law has been applied correctly;
- presenting a case in correspondence, and in person, with the taxpayer or their professional advisers, accountants or lawyers.

Source: Prospects – the UK's official graduate careers website

(www.prospects.ac.uk).

Sometimes the profession seems almost glamorous. In 2007, a Russian tax inspector admitted that he had been recruited by MI6 to spy for Britain. Unmarried mothers, Russian spies... what next? Footballers' wives? Tax investigators are clearly ripe to be the subject of movies written by a range of authors stretching from John le Carré to Jackie Collins.

The job description shown here does not seem specifically designed to attract single mothers or aspiring spies. But there is no doubt that the job has considerably more glamour than in the past.

Once upon a time inspectors were like a favourite uncle, and clever with it. Nowadays investigators are being toughened up by the Customs & Excise gang, a different breed recruited separately to pursue Her Majesty's

interests in gathering indirect taxes. The Customs & Excise gang are more like bovver boys, spending much of their time in bonded warehouses and the holds of cargo ships. There is a sub-plot eventually to integrate the two authorities fully, but the plot is as yet unfolding slowly. The formal merger between the two was merely a first step.

Tax investigators have also been toughened up by a change in the regulations. HMRC is now no longer a preferential creditor when taxpayers or their businesses

go bust. In the old days, being a preferential creditor allowed inspectors to queue in a gentlemanly manner, knowing they were assured of a place near the front. Now they have to make a grab, along with every other creditor, for whatever they can get their hands on.

Nevertheless, for most of the time investigators behave like normal human beings. And they get upset like normal human beings. One case, which went all the way to the High Court, was started because a taxpayer nearly mowed an investigator down with a Rolls-Royce emblazoned with personalised number plates. In *Taxman*, investigators meet people in pubs and restaurants, they make friends while on holiday abroad, and they admire expensively renovated houses. Of course, they also overhear the barman asking his customer, 'How much do you want me to put on the receipt?'

Whistleblowers

Whistleblowers feature regularly in such stories. Whistle-blowing is a complicated act that continues to fascinate psychotherapists and filmmakers. *Silkwood* and *Erin Brockovich* were the stories of two female whistleblowers (many more of them are women than men), and they could well be followed by a movie in the *Taxman* series where the star part is that of a whistleblower. (In the two earlier films, the title roles were taken by Meryl Streep and Julia Roberts respectively. *Taxman's* producers would not be content with anyone less than Angelina Jolie or Nicole Kidman.)

In the UK, there is a hotline number for whistleblowers to call, and since 1890 HMRC has been entitled to give them a reward for their efforts. The UK authorities famously paid £100,000 to a former employee of a bank in Liechtenstein for the names of about 100 UK account holders at his bank. The employee, now in hiding, was a serial informer. He also sold information to the German authorities.

Another whistleblower confessed that, as an employee of the Swiss bank UBS, he helped several US citizens avoid tax. For one client, he is alleged to have smuggled diamonds into the United States by hiding them inside a toothpaste tube. UBS is reported already to have passed information on 320 of its clients to the American authorities.

The US Department of Justice subsequently charged the bank's head of global wealth management (a Swiss citizen) with concealing from the Internal Revenue Service (IRS) – the American equivalent of HMRC – $20 billion-worth of assets belonging to 17,000 US clients. The banker is alleged to have referred to his US business as 'toxic waste' because of its potential to poison the atmosphere. The fall-out from this particular explosion has not yet stopped spreading.

Many whistleblowers are happy to tell their tale for nothing, believing that their righteous behaviour is its own reward. But it is a risky route to follow. A disturbingly large number of them then feel unappreciated for what they have done, and subsequently suffer from depression and/or alcoholism. Other whistleblowers talk for less noble reasons. Taxpayers, for instance, will sometimes, when under interrogation by HMRC's investigators, be tempted to say: 'Well, I'm not the only one doing it. If I tell you about Justin down the road, will you let me off?'

In tax cases, whistleblowers tend to live close to

home, in the guise of aggrieved spouses or employees, competitors, jealous neighbours or jilted lovers. Jilted lovers often have the attitude that if their former partner is going to live without them, then that partner is going to live without lots of other things besides. These include items like the undeclared offshore income that may in the past have enabled the informer to spend long and frequent holidays in places like Marbella and Monte Carlo, dressed in a style to which he or she has since had to become unaccustomed.

Former spouses are also prone to blow the whistle. Things that were hidden from the taxman during a marriage can suddenly be flushed out into the open when the couple are seeking a divorce settlement. In one case, a husband claimed to HMRC that the house where he and his wife lived was owned by an offshore company. But when they came to court to seek a divorce, the wife managed to prove that the house belonged to her husband and that half of it was therefore hers.

HMRC was particularly interested to read the divorce

judge's statement that, 'by virtue of some transaction not explained, or not properly explained, the husband was able to assemble offshore monies which later he deployed in the purchase'. Such judgments, in general, are confidential. But in this case the wife's brother felt moved to bring the judgment to the attention of HMRC.

Finally, don't forget 'anon'. He or she may have a starring role in the *Taxman* movie. HMRC does not ignore information merely because it does not know who's supplying it. *Taxman* may well have its Watergate moment.

Your family

You may love them to bits right now, but after a tax investigation you might want to tear them to bits. Investigations can last for 12 months and more, and they put tremendous pressure on relationships. Indeed, they endure longer than many relationships.

Even with the best will in the world, family members will not be able to see the situation in the same light as you. And in the many cases where the best will in the world is not in evidence, family members may see advantages for themselves in your distress. Spouses, for instance, who are dreaming of greater independence, may want to establish rights to hitherto hidden assets.

And as for the children: well, the possibilities with them are countless. For a start, there is their inheritance to think of. And then maybe they feel that their trust funds are coming under threat. That is enough to put the fear of God into some. And once that fear has spread there is no accounting for what they might do. So never involve children. They never did understand you properly, and they are not going to begin to do so now.

Finally, remember that your mother-in-law is not automatically on your side.

Friends

The stars of this movie never chat about their affairs (tax or otherwise) with 'friends' at the golf club or in the pub. The more you offload your woes on to another person, the more that person in turn needs to offload them on to someone else. Before you know where you are the whole town is familiar with the details of your case. And there is a strong possibility that within that town there lives at least one tax official.

Since the popular television series of the same name, there has been a widespread belief that your friends are, in fact, your nearest and your dearest. Don't believe it. Much better to go back a bit further in the history of communications and stick with the wartime advice: 'Careless Talk Costs Lives' and 'Silence Means Security'. Letting a former flat-mate know that you paid for your house in the Dordogne with cash is not literally going to kill you. But it may cost you the chance of getting a good deal with the taxman should he begin investigating your affairs.

Many taxpayers have found to their cost that the worst kind of friend is a reporter. And today that includes almost anyone who writes a blog or broadcasts information on internet services via the likes of YouTube or Facebook. Tax investigators are just as technologically capable as the rest of us, and they can Google the internet too.

There have been times, however, when they have been a bit floppy with their discs. In 2007 they managed to lose data on 25 million people, all the members of the 7.25 million families that were then entitled to receive child benefits. Members of Parliament were said to have 'gasped' in the House of Commons when the Chancellor of the Exchequer informed them of the loss and advised the 25 million to monitor their bank accounts carefully 'for unusual activity'. The missing disc was never found. No one, however, should work on the assumption that HMRC is going to lose the background information relating to their particular case. Such instances are rare.

A cool and early analysis of problems is the key to a successful conclusion. And that is best done at arm's length with a professional adviser to assist you. It cannot be done with someone you just met on a flight back from New York, nor with someone you shared a flat with once upon a time in the 1980s.

Dead men

This film is not a murder mystery; death is not central to the plot of *The Taxman Always Rings Twice*. But it still might occur. The stress of an investigation can accelerate it, and so can involvement in some of the big-stakes carousel frauds (see page 57), which attract organised crime and its methods. In the film, however, dead men have one big advantage. They don't have to bear the stress of the investigation. Nor has HMRC found a way to interview them. Not surprisingly, HMRC likes its characters to carry on with their lives, settle their dues, and then earn more money – so they can pay yet more into Her Majesty's coffers. (Watch out for the forthcoming *Taxman* movie: *On Her Majesty's Secret Sources*.)

Ghosts

Finally, there is a rather ethereal character who turns up on occasions in *Taxman* movies. Sometimes he goes by the name of Mickey Mouse. On other occasions he is known as John Lennon or Bert Einstein. He is the fictitious employee listed on payrolls merely in order to pad out a company's expenses, reduce its profits and thereby reduce its tax bill.

The tax due on Bert Einstein's fictional income does not worry the unscrupulous employer unduly. For some employers, PAYE, the Pay-as-You-Earn imposition of tax on employees, is known as PAYP: Pay-as-You-Please. Unscrupulous employers please themselves by not paying it.

The locations

Offshore

This is a place that features heavily in all *Taxman* movies. For a tax investigator, it is a bit like a red rag to a bull, home to all sorts of things that he has come to mistrust, things like offshore trusts, offshore accounts and CFCs. (These CFCs are not chlorofluorocarbons, the dangerous stuff that depletes the ozone layer, but rather Controlled Foreign Companies, which flash almost as many danger signals to a tax investigator because they can so easily be used to conceal untaxed income.)

A taxpayer with an offshore anything is liable to come under suspicion and may be subject to an investigation. HMRC tends to forget that some people have offshore accounts for genuine reasons. Sailors, for example, are literally offshore for most of their working lives. And there are in fact real builders who live on the island of Jersey and have bank accounts there. The place is not inhabited entirely by cows and trusts.

Enquiries into a taxpayer's overseas affairs can be

gruelling. In the first place they can take for ever. Getting overseas banks, for instance, to certify interest or dividend payments can be like pulling teeth from a rhino. And international postal services are not all as excellent as they are in London SW1.

Offshore features increasingly in tax cases these days because people travel further and businesses are more global. When tax rates got too high in the UK in times past, people who wanted to escape looked no further than Monaco or Malta. Now they think about moving to an apartment in Thailand or a condo in Phoenix, Arizona. The world is literally their oyster.

Businesses, whatever their size, are also going global. The world, said Thomas Friedman, a *New York Times* columnist, is flat. But one thing he was not referring to was the rate of tax. There is no flat rate around the world. Rates differ greatly. So big businesses and little businesses alike try to structure themselves so that they pay a minimum of tax when all their operations are taken into account.

For American companies, that often means having a registered office in the state of Delaware. For Europeans, it almost invariably involves something Dutch – often, indeed, something double Dutch: a headquarters in Rotterdam, say, and a finance subsidiary in the Netherlands Antilles.

Certain places have purposely set themselves up as 'tax havens' with the specific aim of attracting the assets of businessmen and rich individuals. Most tax havens are small countries with few natural resources other than pretty views of mountains or beaches: think Andorra and the British Virgin Islands. They try to boost their revenues by attracting money in search of secrecy, for they can see how lucrative the business has been for places such as Switzerland and Liechtenstein. In the movie, you may be able to spot a couple of Picassos on the walls of a Liechtenstein law firm. (And this is not some flight of fancy by the props department.)

Life, however, is becoming increasingly difficult for these offshore centres or so-called tax havens. A spate of information-sharing agreements between countries has meant that fewer and fewer of them remain tax 'heavens'. Among the member states of the Organisation for Economic Cooperation and Development (OECD), few are still defined by the OECD as 'uncooperative tax regimes' – i.e. places that do not share information with other member states. Two that are still in the category are Andorra and Monaco – although both countries made it clear in April 2009 that they intended to rapidly implement the standards of transparency and effective exchange of information that would move them off the OECD's list.

Your adviser's office

This is a place for the dispensation of tea and sympathy. There may be a market for a book that ranks the quality of professional tax advisers' biscuits. For these are powerful competitive weapons in the fight against tax investigators.

Advisers' offices are places to let off steam, to tell the truth, the whole truth and nothing but the truth as it appears to you, the taxpayer. Even at their most modern, the offices consist of a warren of small meeting rooms where clients can be discreetly interviewed and where they can find a sympathetic shoulder to cry on. And, as they are almost always based near the centre of large cities, tax advisers' offices can also be a convenient springboard for a visit to an exhibition or a bit of serious shopping.

The investigator's office

Investigators are spread around a number of offices. There are so-called 'local' offices, which deal with the vast majority of tax affairs (though they are not necessarily local to the individual taxpayer). And then there are specialist offices which deal with particular industries. The entertainment industry, for instance, has a special office based in Gateshead, across the River Tyne from Newcastle. And then there is the Specialist Investigations (SI) unit – formerly known as Special Civil Investigations (SCI) – an elite squad of tax investigators that is rolled out to deal with serious cases wherever they arise.

Visits to investigators should be kept to an absolute minimum. There is a scene in the movie where, just as a taxpayer reaches the street outside an investigator's office, he starts to jump for joy. The camera pans across to an upstairs window of the office building he has just left. There, an investigator is standing stock still as he watches the antics below.

Also avoid, whenever possible, visiting pubs within walking distance of any HMRC office. There is always the possibility that investigators are having an internal review meeting at one and the same time as you are celebrating and offering champagne all round.

Home

This is the place where you and your family seek refuge in this time of trouble. It should be a peaceful haven with no valuable paintings on the walls and absolutely no expensive cars visible in the drive. It is certainly not a place in which to conduct interviews with tax investigators. You go to them; don't let them come to you.

Ideally, meetings should be held in an adviser's office. But an investigator may come knocking on your door in any case and take a look at your home. Investigators are quite good at digging for information. They might spot the annex that you claim was built as a granny flat. Why, for instance, is granny not living there when you allege she paid for it? And did she also pay for the brand new swimming pool where the kids are screaming with joy as the investigator turns in to the gravel drive?

On the day the investigators come, persuade the rest of the family to go and see granny. And, dammit, let them take the Porsche.

Jail

Jail is an unlikely destination for the stars of this movie. But Lester Piggott, the jockey, went there for tax evasion, and so did Al Capone. Indeed there is a trend today, when investigators suspect taxpayers of serious criminal offences, of pursuing them with tax charges because they feel it gives them the best chance of putting them behind bars. This was notoriously the way they got Al Capone, and cases like that have become known as 'Al Capone cases'.

Some tax offenders are more likely than others to end up in prison. Lawyers and accountants for instance (people who definitely should know better); repeat offenders; and people with words like Vanuatu or Andorra on their letter heading. There is a popular saying: 'Clients go to jail; lawyers go to lunch.' Among tax offenders it is more likely to be the other way round.

In one recent six-month period, HMRC issued only

three press releases about prosecutions. They were headed:

- 'Tax credit cheat sentenced to community service.'
- 'Unqualified accountant sentenced to 12 months for cheating.'
- 'Tax cheat barrister loses appeal against jail sentence.'

Although the tax barrister was convicted of cheating for his own account, rather than being involved in the cheating of his clients, it did not help his case (nor his sentencing – he got four and a half years) that he was a member of the bar. The professionals are sure to get heavier sentences.

Sentences have in general been increasing in recent years. In one case in 2001 a judge said that the appropriate sentence for a large-scale effort to cheat HMRC was between four and eight years in prison.

'Oh what a tangled web we weave when first we practise to deceive,' wrote the poet Sir Walter Scott in what has become one of HMRC's favourite quotations. Even the most innocent lies can rebound in unexpected ways. In the movie, for instance, there is a taxpayer who tells HMRC that £250,000 is the absolute limit of what he can afford. But then he boasts about town and at the golf club that he is going to settle for £500,000 'and it'll be a really good deal'. Unfortunately for him, two of the people he tells about this 'really good deal' later give evidence about what he has said. His big mouth lands him in big trouble.

There are five simple ways to avoid going to jail:

- Don't lie to HMRC.
- Don't lie to HMRC.
- Don't lie to HMRC.
- Don't lie to HMRC.
- Don't lie to HMRC.

The props

Boats and planes

The costume department is very important in *Taxman* movies. Taxpayers dress carefully for their meetings with investigators. They leave their Patek Philippe watches at home and they plonk their Oyster cards clearly on the table when they walk in. They make absolutely sure they do not arrive in a chauffeur-driven car with personalised number plates.

Investigators take a strange delight in perusing magazines with pictures and stories about the rich and famous. They have an almost unhealthy fascination with lists of the owners of private planes and of large yachts. Some generous companies go so far as to buy boats and planes for their top people to enjoy, but these may be mentioned in their annual reports.

Companies will insist that such bits of precious metal are absolutely essential for business purposes. Their top executives simply cannot function without them. But there is an almost direct correlation between a

corporate executive's view of his own status within his company and his desire to float around inside a Lear jet. Upon promotion, his idea of an ego trip swiftly becomes a flight at several thousand feet accompanied by a Fortnum's hamper and someone else's secretary.

It is all too easy to push the boat (or the plane) out too far. Boats and planes can very quickly give rise to a taxable charge. For tax purposes, the benefit of such means of transport is considered to go with their availability, not their use. It is not a good strategy to leave corporate jets hanging around in hangars.

If a yacht is owned by a company and is effectively available at all times to the chief executive, then that CEO will be deemed to have benefited in each year to the tune of 20 per cent of the higher of the market value (when the yacht was first provided) and the cost of the yacht. If the yacht cost £5 million (and that is not a large sum these days when you consider that the *Maltese Falcon* – a super-super-yacht built by the Silicon Valley venture capitalist Tom Perkins – cost something in the region of $300 million), there is £1 million a year of deemed benefit, not to mention the maintenance costs and the cost of the crew.

Neither the managing director nor his captain need ever to have set foot on the thing's immaculate teak deck for it to give rise to a huge tax bill. The only escape is to charter the vessel. When it is chartered to someone else then the boat (or plane) is genuinely not available to the executive and cannot therefore give rise to a taxable benefit.

Safe deposit boxes

Several scenes from the next *Taxman* movie were shot in and around safe-deposit boxes in central London. In 2008, the police raided a number of locations and gained access to over 6,700 boxes. From the raids (code-named Operation Rize) they seized works of art, guns and cash worth over £50 million, much of it kept in supermarket carrier bags.

The cash and the caribou

One real-life story (rejected as a *Taxman* script because it was deemed to be too unbelievable) concerned a UK taxpayer who was being questioned by HMRC about a possible fraud. One of the taxman's favourite questions in such circumstances is: 'What is the maximum amount of cash you would have held at any one time?' Typically, the question elicits responses ranging from a few hundred to a few thousand pounds. But this taxpayer shocked all those assembled at the interview with his immediate and unflinching response: 'Five million dollars,' he said.

The man explained that one of his roles was to act as a 'fixer' for a hugely wealthy Middle Eastern businessman. His job was to smooth the passage of the businessman's entourage across Europe with the help of cash dispensed from a briefcase. The deal was that the briefcase would contain $5 million at the beginning of a trip, and the taxpayer's incentive for keeping the entourage (and in particular the businessman's two errant sons) out of trouble was that anything left in the briefcase at the end of the trip was his to keep.

The man then produced a scribbled record of out-of-pocket expenses that he had incurred. One note appeared to refer to £2,500 that had been spent on 'livestock', and the question then arose as to how this fitted into the man's role as a fixer.

In reply, he explained that his employer had recently acquired an estate in England known as Caribou Lodge. But the Middle Eastern businessman did not know what a caribou was, so he asked his fixer to enlighten him. Having been told that it was some kind of deer, the employer demanded that some be found immediately to populate his new acquisition.

Ever resourceful, the fixer ensured that fifteen red deer had taken up residence on the estate by the time the businessman and his family next came for a visit. After some research by HMRC of crime reports in local papers up and down the country it became apparent that the deer had been rustled from a sanctuary in Scotland and transported down the A1 to Caribou Lodge. Oh dear!

The police obtained the right to 'search and seize' the contents of the boxes under the Proceeds of Crime Act, 2002 (POCA), a piece of legislation designed to help in cases of suspected criminal money laundering. However, the police clearly did not suspect that all the boxes in this case contained proceeds of crime. (Indeed, they soon returned over 900 to their owners without further ado.) The case raised the question as to whether the police were acting beyond their powers in searching every box.

Information from the raids was passed on to HMRC and led to subsequent investigations. While it was perhaps never very likely that the police would actually prosecute taxpayers for tax evasion where there was no wider criminality, that option was always on the cards for HMRC. In order to escape jail, at least one safe-deposit-box owner was induced to confess to HMRC and apologise for his misdemeanours. As he did so he was heard to mumble: 'Better sorry than safe.'

Cash

Cash features prominently in the movie – not Johnny Cash, nor even Joaquim Phoenix (who played the country-music singer in the movie of his life), but greenbacks, lolly, loot. Large amounts of cash are almost always suspicious to an investigator. In the age of internet banking, credit cards and money-laundering legislation, there are fewer and fewer legitimate uses for cash in daily life.

Everyone knows that the builder who is prepared to give his client a discount 'for cash' can do so only because, when paid in cash, he will be able to avoid paying VAT.

Not only is cash highly inflammable and vulnerable to theft, but it is also prone to other less obvious risks. One tax evader, who for years kept a stash of cash in a safe-deposit box – and away from the taxman's beady eye – found that he had to swap all his notes for new ones as and when they were withdrawn from circulation. The logistics involved in taking Tesco bags full of notes from a safe-deposit box to a bank in order to change them were demanding. The ultimate in 'cash and carry'!

The one that got away

In one raid on a taxpayer's house, the investigators, the suspect, his adviser and the police were all sitting round a table when HMRC asked the taxpayer if they could see some documents. The suspect said he'd go and fetch them.

When the man had not returned after fifteen minutes, the police and the investigators realised he'd done a bunk. What's more, he'd locked them all in the room. And he'd taken the documents in question along with him as he made his escape across the roof. The police missed him at Heathrow by about an hour. Needless to say, the documents all disappeared.

The jargon

Carousel

This is the title of a big-hit movie about Customs & Excise. The title comes from the name given to a plot behind a complicated Customs & Excise investigation. In the story, a budding criminal buys small high-value items in bulk from abroad – in this particular case mobile phones from Belgium. (The film managed to stay within budget by being filmed entirely on location in low-cost Lithuania – another place from which items may be bought by the tax-avoiding trader.) The criminal brings the goods quite openly into the UK, where they are zero-rated for VAT since they come from within the EU. (Belgium is a full member.)

The importer then sells the goods within the UK to a number of different companies under his control in order to help disguise their origin. (This churning is the so-called 'carousel'.) In the meanwhile, he adds VAT and scarpers with the tax (to somewhere way beyond the borders even of Belgium or Lithuania). The goods are

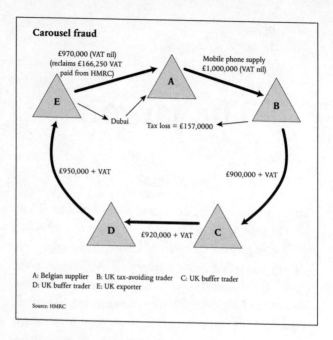

Carousel fraud

£970,000 (VAT nil)
(reclaims £166,250 VAT
paid from HMRC)

E

Dubai

Mobile phone supply
£1,000,000 (VAT nil)

A

B

Tax loss = £157,0000

£950,000 + VAT

£900,000 + VAT

D

£920,000 + VAT

C

A: Belgian supplier   B: UK tax-avoiding trader   C: UK buffer trader
D: UK buffer trader   E: UK exporter

Source: HMRC

eventually sold by someone else (who may or may not be innocent of the scam) to the final consumer.

In the movie, the criminal – who starts life as a bouncer at a nightclub somewhere in the north of England – gets away with several million pounds which he spends on a house in Virgin Gorda and a couple of Ferraris. (It was a particular challenge for the film crew to recreate a corner of Virgin Gorda within the borders of Lithuania.) Similar scams have been known to involve unpaid taxes of anything up to £100 million. One estimate suggests that HMRC lost over £1.3 billion from such schemes in 2005 alone.

After a few unsuccessful attempts to pursue the criminals involved in these scams directly, HMRC has changed tack. Its new strategy is to deny the final vendor's claim for repayment of VAT on the goods, and it has won some 50 per cent of the relevant cases heard so far. HMRC is arguing that its first responsibility is to protect revenue; the pursuit of criminals comes second, and is anyway the responsibility of others.

Evasion and avoidance

The difference between tax evasion and tax avoidance was once said to be the thickness of a prison wall. The one was assuredly illegal (tax evasion); the other (tax avoidance) was what you did when you stuck to the letter, if not the spirit of the law. Nowadays things are not so straightforward. Governments have on occasions confused the two terms for their own political purposes – suggesting they are introducing measures in order to clamp down on criminals when the measures are in fact designed to discourage tax avoidance.

There is a form of hardcore tax evasion that remains clear and indisputable – for example, where some sort of dishonesty is involved, especially the non-disclosure of relevant facts or the creation of fake documents. But around that hard core there is now a vast penumbra of

"I suppose they've each got 'TAX' round at the back of the collar" said Alice to herself.

uncertainty where it is not possible any longer clearly to distinguish avoidance from evasion.

In 2005 the UK's chief inspector of taxes said that he was going to get rid of the distinction between the two altogether so that we could all talk instead about degrees of compliance. But the expressions are too well embedded in tax talk for them to be removed by mere decree.

The French have managed to muddy the waters in this area – not, of course, for the first time where the English are concerned – by choosing to use the expres-

Spectrum of compliant and non-compliant behaviour
Behaviours and corresponding HMRC action

Getting it right	Attempt to comply, but make mistakes	Don't take reasonable care	Deliberate non-compliance	Deliberate non-compliance which merits criminal investigation
Normal HMRC process/review	Enquiry/ investigation	Enquiry/ investigation Imposition of penalties	Enquiry/ investigation Imposition of penalties	Enquiry/ investigation Imposition of penalties Prosecution
✓	✗	✗✗	✗✗✗	GO TO JAIL?

NB: HMRC no longer refer to avoidance or evasion, but only to the level of compliance in the behaviour of the taxpayer.

sion '*evasion fiscal*' when they mean 'tax avoidance'. This provides ample opportunity for misunderstanding in the international forums that, in this age of globalisation, are increasingly influential in framing tax legislation.

Reducing your tax bill to a minimum while sticking to the spirit of the law is called tax mitigation, and no one objects to that. By creating things like tax-free savings certificates from National Savings & Investments (NS&I), the government in some cases positively encourages it. But creating devices that are set up purely for the purpose of avoiding tax is becoming increasingly objectionable and can get you into trouble.

The field of evasion and avoidance is even more full

of pitfalls for companies than it is for individuals. They are under an obligation to their shareholders to keep their costs down. So they have a different purpose in seeking to find ways in which they can lower their tax bill. Several landmark cases, however, have clarified that any scheme that lacks 'a business purpose' will be struck down and the tax bill calculated as if it were not in place.

Despite this, there are still plenty of people eager to advise taxpayers on ways in which they can reduce the amount of tax they pay. Some of the ways that such people recommend are perfectly legal; but some of them are not. America's IRS warns taxpayers not to fall victim to tax scams, and it lists eight that are particularly common. 'Taxpayers need to remember,' says the IRS, 'that if it sounds too good to be true, it probably is.'

Money laundering

This is an expression popularised by the story of our old friend Al Capone, the Chicago gangster who used his laundry businesses to clean his dirty money as well as his dirty linen. Legislation aimed at making money-laundering more difficult was introduced into many countries after the terrorist attacks at the turn of the 21st century.

Ostensibly, such legislation was designed to help in the pursuit of international terrorists, arms dealers and drug traffickers by cutting them off from their sources of finance. Since these are essentially cash businesses, the legislation was aimed at preventing large cash transactions from passing through the financial system.

It goes without saying that few terrorists or drug dealers fill in their tax returns honestly, if they fill them in at all. Hence most money-laundering cases involve large amounts of unpaid tax. The two activities – tax avoidance and money laundering – have become increasingly intertwined. Press articles, for example, talk about 'government measures to crack down on money laundering and tax avoidance' as if the two were inseparable.

There is no doubt that the focus on money-laundering legislation has changed attitudes to tax avoidance. And it sometimes seems as if the authorities want to suggest that anyone avoiding tax must be involved in money laundering, if they are not actually a real live terrorist. This is, of course, complete bunkum.

SARs and CARs

It is now mandatory for any professional-services firm in the UK (lawyers, accountants, bankers, brokers and so on) to supply the authorities with a Suspicious Activity Report (SAR) whenever they suspect that one of their clients may have been up to no good. These reports are automatically made available to HMRC. Estate agents are among the firms that have to supply such reports, so news of large houses bought for cash is sure to reach HMRC's ears.

CAR stands for Charities, Assets and Residence, a special department within HMRC that deals with these three aspects of tax and a number of others besides. including:

- savings and audit;
- inheritance tax;
- pension schemes;
- trusts;
- capital gains;

- employee shares and securities;
- share assets valuation.

Charities are increasingly being used as vehicles for tax evasion. Money allegedly collected to buy sunhats in Spain for donkeys has on occasions been used to buy sunny flats in Spain, not for donkeys but for the mistress of the charity's chairman.

The whole area of capital gains is a minefield for the unwary. Whereas a taxpayer's income is relatively smooth, year on year, capital gains tend to come in big one-off blobs, and these tend to flash warning signals on HMRC's computers. It is always wise for taxpayers who are about to realise a large capital gain to seek professional advice.

By the way, don't waste too much brain capacity remembering HMRC's departmental acronyms. What was a CAR this month may be a BUS next month. HMRC seems to change them about every six months. In *Taxman: Part 2* they're sure to be different from what they were in this, the opening episode.

SI

This is another of HMRC's acronyms that has been changed recently. What used to be known as the Special Compliance Office (the SCO), then the Special Civil Investigations office (the SCI), is now known as Specialist

Investigations (SI). This is the HMRC department called in when there is a suspicion of significant tax evasion or significant tax avoidance. It is the special force, the glamorous part of the business, the part that novelists and film directors are automatically drawn to first.

SI enquiries progress according to what is known as Code of Practice 8 if tax avoidance is the issue. But cases of suspected fraud or evasion follow Code of Practice 9 and are governed by something that used to be referred to as the 'Hansard Rules' (named after the official published report of British parliamentary proceedings). Since the Inland Revenue was merged with Customs & Excise these have been replaced by the Civil Investigation of Fraud procedure (CIF). The CIF procedure lays down a series of formal questions – five in cases of direct tax; four for indirect tax.

Once a taxpayer has been offered the CIF procedure under Code of Practice 9, he or she cannot be prosecuted for the tax offence. It is possible, however, still to be prosecuted for lying, for making false statements, or for providing false documents.

Trustworthy

For years, trusts have been used as a means to shelter income and capital gains from tax. They have a similar effect on a tax investigator's nostrils as the word 'offshore'. They make him smell a rat. Particularly offensive is the offshore trust.

UK trusts that owe tax on income or gains have a responsibility to notify HMRC. The trustees will need to file a self-assessment tax return to report trust income and gains. Anyone who puts property into a UK trust has an obligation to notify HMRC on the creation of that trust.

Foreign trusts – those where some or all of the trustees are not UK resident – are not created or administered under UK law. But they may trigger a UK tax charge under complex anti-avoidance rules, and HMRC

Some valid reasons for setting up a trust

- To look after assets for minors and to provide income for their education and welfare.
- To protect assets in certain special circumstances – for example, a potential divorce.
- To enable one beneficiary to enjoy income, but for the underlying capital to be retained for others.
- To make arrangements for the members of your family, including future additions.
- To help with tax planning – for example a 'will trust' can reduce inheritance tax liability.
- For making gifts – because you can specify in what circumstances beneficiaries will receive those gifts.
- To protect assets when you do not want the beneficiary to have full control over them.
- For social reasons (e.g. to have something to brag about at the golf club).

will then need to be notified and paid accordingly. UK beneficiaries of foreign trusts need to be especially careful and should seek expert advice.

There are also special types of UK trusts with their own sets of tax rules – such as charities, pension funds, unit trusts and employee share schemes.

Trust us – it's a minefield.

Even more offensive to the taxman than offshore trusts are things like *stiftungs* (don't ask) and *anstalts*. These are rare specimens in the trust world, believed to survive only in Liechtenstein. They are a mix between a company and a trust, and their main advantage is that they make it very difficult for outsiders to find out who are the beneficiaries of the assets that they hold. An *anstalt* has no members, no participants and no shareholders.

Whatever the genetic purpose of these rare specimens, they are sure to drive a taxman (and especially an American taxman) completely crazy should he come across one. They have been put firmly on the list of endangered fiscal species.

The plot

Although the title of the movie suggests that the plot begins with a knock on the door, most investigations begin with a letter (see overleaf for a typical example). This is sometimes known as a 'Mae West' letter because it suggests that someone will come and see you some time.

On first reading, the letter may sound bland. But don't be fooled. It suggests that there is a discrepancy in some aspect of the self-assessment returns on which your tax bills have been calculated. This is no laughing matter. Although some taxpayers are selected entirely at random for such an investigation, the vast majority are chosen for a reason.

Occasionally, HMRC decides to look closely at one particular group of people. Not all that long ago, for instance, it chose to cast its beady eye on professional football players. One test case involved a top England player who was attempting to establish that the sum paid by his club for his 'image rights' – the money paid for allowing

HMRC

Etc

Dear Sir

Thank you for your Tax Return for the year ended 5 April 20xx. I am writing to tell you that I intend to make some enquiries into this return. I have written to your tax adviser, BDO Stoy Hayward LLP, to ask for the information I need.

I enclose a copy of our Code of Practice. It explains how we make enquiries and how we keep our promise of fair treatment under HMRC's Service Commitment to you.

When you have read the leaflet, please contact me if you require further information.

Yours faithfully

HM Inspector of Taxes

his face to appear on the back of a T-shirt, for example – could be separated from his regular salary. If it could, then the club would be free to pay it into a separate company, and it could be treated separately for tax purposes.

Thereafter the plot unfolds according to a series of deadlines. For example, the 'Mae West' letter has to be sent within 12 months of the due date of filing the tax return – normally by the end of January each year. So anyone who did not receive a letter by 31 January 2010 concerning their tax liability for the year 2007/08 cannot be subject to a random enquiry.

But don't imagine that failing to file a return in time lets you completely off the hook. Penalties are imposed when deadlines are not met. Also, HMRC can open an enquiry at any time within the next 20 years should it come across hitherto undiscovered material information or serious fraud. A tax return, however late it is filed, is clearly material.

A remake of this movie in years to come may be called *The Taxman Always E-mails Twice*. But for the moment, investigators are using e-mail and other electronic communications only on rare occasions when other types of communication are particularly difficult. Note, however, that when they do use it, they add a return slip which advises them that the e-mail has been opened. This eliminates the possibility of an electronic version of 'the dog ate it' (see page 99) or 'it got lost in the post'. 'It got mauled by a virus' will not work.

Major deadlines

31 October: for submission of a paper tax return
If the paper return arrives after this deadline you will
be charged an automatic £100 penalty.

31 January: for submission of on-line tax returns
If it arrives after this deadline you will be charged an
automatic £100 penalty.

**31 January: for payment of any balance of tax
you owe for the tax year to the previous 5 April**
Daily interest is charged on payments received after
this date. You may be asked to make a first 'payment
on account' for the current tax year.

28 February
If you still have not paid the balance due by 31
January, you will be charged an automatic 5 per cent
surcharge on top of the amount still owing. This is in
addition to any interest payments.

31 July
If you are due to make payments on account, this is
the deadline for making a second 'payment on
account' for tax owing for the preceding tax year.

If you still owe tax that you were due to pay by the
previous 31 January, you'll be charged a second automatic
5 per cent surcharge on top of the amount you owe.

There is a whole range of additional deadlines for
employers' compliance with PAYE, VAT and
corporation tax.

From here on there are six sub-plots to the movie – first there is the revelation, followed by the information, the preparation, the duration, the negotiation and then the mitigation. All six come together in one grand final denouement – the termination.

The revelation

Volunteering information may help to secure a better deal with HMRC. But the information given should

never be partial. Some people think that they can get away with disclosing only a part of the earnings that they have stashed abroad. If that is what you want to do, you are better off not volunteering to disclose at all. HMRC has a duty to check everything anyway. They are very likely to look into the things that you don't tell them about.

And don't assume that they won't look into the smallest details. There is a case in the movie where an investigator is looking through a business's records and he notices that the address on an invoice from a cleaner has been spelt incorrectly. He also notices that the name of the cleaner is rather unusual. On visiting the address, the investigator is greeted by two elderly sisters who have lived at the property for over sixty years and have never heard of the so-called 'cleaner'. The investigator's suspicions are further aroused when he realises that the cleaner's name, 'R. Shastay', is an anagram of 'ashtrays'.

The volunteering of information became more popular after HMRC forced a number of the country's biggest banks to reveal the names of those UK customers who had overseas accounts. Having gathered the information, HMRC then sent out more than 5,000 letters to the holders of such accounts, and it plans to send out yet more.

Some people with overseas accounts decided to try and make a virtue out of what looked increasingly like a necessity. So they volunteered information to HMRC before they were compelled to volunteer it. There is, of course, nothing wrong with being a UK resident and having a bank account outside the UK. Non-doms, for instance, (see page 21) can in certain circumstances keep income from abroad in such accounts free of tax as long as they do not remit it to the UK. And even where there is avoidance, it is sometimes innocent. There have been cases of overseas accounts inherited by widows who were genuinely not aware that their deceased husband's overseas foundations were mostly cosmetic.

The information

Information is the life-blood of all investigations and HMRC collects it from a number of sources – from informers, from international exchanges of information, from surveillance operations, and from its own online hotline – www.taxevasionhotline.co.uk. It also shares information these days with a number of other government agencies, including the police, the Charity Commission, and the Serious Fraud Office.

For some time it has had powers to demand that tax-payers hand over documents. These powers (as laid down in section 20 of the 1970 Taxes Management Act) have remained virtually unchanged for decades. With them, the taxman can obtain a warrant to search premises and to seize documents.

The definition of what constitutes a 'document' has been updated for the modern era. It is now considered to be 'anything in which information of any description is recorded'. That, the taxman has made clear, includes hard discs, floppy discs, CDs and any other electronic method of storage.

Increasingly, authorities in different countries co-operate in exchanging information. Australia, Canada, Japan, the UK and the US have set up something called the Joint International Tax Shelter Information Centre (JITSIC), an organisation where they share information on tax shelters and the firms that plan and promote them. The European Savings Directive gives all EU tax author-

ities access to details of interest earned by residents from financial institutions in almost all other EU member states. On top of which, many countries have double-taxation agreements that allow for exchanges of information relevant to tax enquiries.

Data-protection legislation has given you, the tax-payer, the right to ask for copies of personal information that HMRC holds about you. But it has not protected the privacy of bank accounts. Information held there is less sacrosanct than it used to be. HMRC recently gained

The official hook, line and sinker

'HMRC has recently used its legal powers to obtain information about holders of offshore accounts from a number of banks.

'HMRC has also obtained similar details through the European Savings Directive, which provides for the exchange of information about interest payable to residents of other countries.

'For a limited period HMRC offered a facility (the Offshore Disclosure Facility) to help offshore account holders to get their tax affairs up to date. This facility is now closed.

'HMRC is now pursuing those with offshore accounts and tax liabilities who did not notify their intention to disclose under the scheme by 22 June 2007, as well as those who notified but decided not to disclose.

'In some cases penalties could amount to 100 per cent of the tax due and in exceptional circumstances criminal investigation may be considered.

'HMRC is now contacting holders of offshore bank accounts who chose not to disclose under the Offshore Disclosure Facility.

'Depending on the circumstances this contact may take the form of:

- a letter and an initial form, followed, where appropriate, by the issue of a disclosure form to enable account holders with unpaid tax to bring their tax affairs up to date;
- a formal notice of enquiry;
- the issue of a self-assessment return for the years where none has been submitted;
- in exceptional circumstances that meet the criteria within our published Criminal Investigation Policy, the undertaking of a criminal investigation.'

Source: HMRC website 2008 (www.hmrc.gov.uk)

In addition, discussions with offshore havens and jurisdictions continue at the highest levels of HMRC and government.

access to the details of the offshore accounts of several big banks' UK customers, and it launched over 11,000 investigations as a result. The authorities now have so much information on account holders (see box on previous pages) that the only question is, how are they going to process it all?

The preparation

Thorough preparation is vital. People don't plan to fail; they fail to plan. And this is particularly true of taxpayers under investigation. Right from the beginning of an investigation, you should be well prepared. That means getting records of your income and expenditure straight, with supporting evidence (such as bank statements) where appropriate.

It also means getting into the right frame of mind. You should be realistic and polite at all times, and should try to put yourself in the place of the investigator. It is no good thinking of the investigation as yet another competition where the aim is to get away with paying the absolute minimum. And there is no point in getting into a rage about the injustice of it all. Remember that the purpose of the whole process is to end up *with* a settlement and *without* a prosecution.

Your adviser will explain how meetings with HMRC should be conducted and will tell you what to expect. This is of paramount importance, since people who go into meetings not knowing what to expect tend to make guesses when questioned under pressure. For most of our life, we all feel a tremendous urge to provide answers.

When under interrogation, taxpayers, like everybody else, tend to talk too much. In the film, one character is asked his name. Instead of answering 'Jim Smith' and then remaining silent, he says:

'Jim Smith.'

Very short pause.

'And I live in Scunthorpe with my wife and two kids, and we never go on holidays abroad. It was my mother-in-law who told me about this chap she met on a plane when she was coming back from Tenerife with our Vicky.

So I rang him and he said it would only cost £5,000. So I paid him in cash which he said was all right because my mother-in-law was a non-dom – which I thought meant she wouldn't touch domestic work, which she wouldn't, of course – and then I didn't pay VAT. But I wouldn't, would I?'

Much better just to tell them your name.

You should always ensure that notes are taken of any meetings that you have with HMRC. Your adviser will do this on your behalf. Where the meeting is the opening meeting of a Code 9 investigation (an investigation of suspected serious fraud), the investigator will send you and your adviser a copy of his notes for your agreement. To tape or film a meeting, either party needs the other's approval.

The duration

The duration of an investigation varies according to the availability of information, the temperament of the players, and the speed with which HMRC can review the adviser's report on the case. The usual time is between six and twelve months, but with technically based cases it can take much longer – if, for example, both sides need to take the advice of tax counsel. When any part of a case has to go to the Commissioners (see page 102), it can stretch out for years.

But don't hope that by spinning it out you are increasing your chances of an amnesty or forgiveness. The Offshore Disclosure Facility (ODF) of 2007, heralded by some as an amnesty, was in fact no such thing. Taxpayers still had to come up with any unpaid tax that was due, plus the interest on it. The carrot was a reduction in the penalty to 10 per cent of the unpaid tax for those declaring income under the terms of the facility.

The ODF raised about £400 million, which is less than HMRC was hoping for. Some still claimed the ODF was a success. But there were, nonetheless, plenty of taxpayers who did not come forward to declare previously undisclosed taxable income. It was also disappointing in that it failed to flush out a high-profile tax case that could have acted as a further deterrent by showing how effective the process had been.

The subsequent offer which was announced by the government in the April 2009 budget made it clear that it would not give such a generous reduction in the penalty. That would only have encouraged taxpayers to wait for the next such deal in the expectation that the penalty would then be even lower.

In general, delaying tactics are less effective today than they used to be. It was once thought that they increased the chances of a good settlement, on the grounds that after a case had dragged on for years some investigator somewhere would eventually decide that it had to be resolved – just to get it off the books. Or, alternatively, he would move on to another department and the case would be ignored by his successor. But today the process is more sophisticated and fairer.

The negotiation

At the heart of every *Taxman* story lies a process of negotiation, a negotiation that takes place between the taxpayer and HMRC. Taxpayers often start by saying: 'I want to see these people. I want this sorted. And I want it sorted now.' But such bullish talk is not helpful. In tax-avoidance cases there is rarely any need for you to meet HMRC directly. Most contact is done by an adviser.

As early in the process as possible, you and your advisers work out a strategy and decide what a reasonable settlement might be. That may have to be modified as information becomes available during the process of the investigation, but defining an end right from the beginning makes it much easier to attain that end.

In a lot of cases, advisers can tell within the very first hour of the very first meeting how the case is going to progress. They cannot forecast the actual outcome, but they get to know the parameters. For a start, your attitude counts for a lot. It does not pay to be too casual. Investigators don't like it, for instance, when they ask a taxpayer about his expenses and he replies: 'Let's say they're about the same as last year.' They also tend to think that taxpayers who protest their innocence the loudest have the most to hide. 'The lady doth protest too much, methinks,' is one of their favourite lines from the Bard, with whose works they are quite familiar.

The bigger cases are more difficult, and a proper plan of how the process is to be managed is essential for

these. The plan should be prepared together with your advisers and with HMRC. Sharing problems with HMRC can sometimes be helpful.

In tax evasion cases there are normally two meetings – a formal interview at the beginning, and a second meeting at the time of the final settlement. At the formal interview, there are usually two investigators present. Be aware that one of them will be watching your body language as much as anything else.

Investigators try to be non-confrontational. But they

hold their cards close to their chest, like players in a game of poker. When they ask about where your children go to school, they are not genuinely interested in the quality of the little ones' education. They want to know what fees are being paid, and how. Although you are under no legal obligation to say anything during the interviews, after a while many taxpayers end up chattering away at will. *Cave* chatterer!

The interview revolves around five formal questions:

1 Have you omitted or incorrectly recorded any transactions in the books of any business with which you have been connected?
2 To the best of your knowledge, are all these books correct and complete?
3 Are the tax returns of all these businesses correct and complete?
4 Are your personal tax returns also correct and complete?
5 Will you allow HMRC to examine your business records, bank statements and personal financial records in order to check that you've given the correct answers to questions 1–4?

If you now live abroad (outside the UK's jurisdiction) and have no assets whatsoever in the UK, then you face a rather different type of negotiation if you come under HMRC's beady eye for allegedly unpaid taxes in previous fiscal years. Your tactic can be: 'Come and get me if you want me.' But you should be aware that you will not be able to return to the UK without the risk of incarceration unless you do eventually reach a settlement.

The mitigation (not litigation)

The climax of the story, if you are found to have sent in incorrect tax returns, is the agreement on a final liability. Too many taxpayers become obsessed with the penalties they might have to pay. The key is to mitigate the tax, because both the interest due and the penalty are determined by it.

The penalty depends on three things:

- the amount of tax 'understated' – i.e. the amount omitted from your return;
- your behaviour in making the understatement;
- the extent to which you are helpful during the investigator's enquiry.

From 1 April 2009, the same regime of penalties now applies across the whole range of taxes and duties – which makes things a bit simpler.

In America penalties of up to 20 per cent of the amount due can be imposed for what is described as 'a substantial understatement of tax'. An understatement is considered to be substantial if it is more than the greater of:

- 10 per cent of the tax required to be shown on the return; or
- $5,000.

In 2008, the actor Nicolas Cage (real name Nicolas Coppola) agreed to pay $666,000 in back taxes and penalties to America's IRS. Between 2002 and 2004, the actor had written off some $3.3 million as business expenses when the money had actually been spent on maintaining his opulent lifestyle, a lifestyle that included a Gulfsteam 1159a turbojet and a Los Angeles pad that he subsequently put on the market for $29 million. The cases of high-profile individuals such as Cage get reported around the world and may have a sobering effect (albeit briefly) on tax evaders everywhere.

Part of the process of negotiation is devoted to trying to reduce the penalties, to making them as small as possible. (Cage's advisers negotiated with the IRS – successfully it seems, since the taxman was originally reported to be seeking $1 million in back taxes excluding interest.) HMRC has considerable discretion in this area. For returns and documents submitted before 1 April 2009 fines could be mitigated by:

- up to 20 per cent for helpful disclosure;

- an additional 10 per cent for voluntary disclosure;
- up to another 40 per cent for cooperation during the enquiry; and
- up to a further 40 per cent depending on the seriousness of the offence.

For returns and documents relating to the period after April 2008, and submitted to HMRC on or after 1 April 2009, a completely new penalty regime applies.

In cases of direct tax, HMRC differentiates between three types of offence – carelessness, deliberate offences, and deliberate offences that are concealed. In an attempt to differentiate between them, investigators are beginning to ask taxpayers for their curriculum vitae to judge what constitutes carelessness in each particular case. It is different, for example, for someone with a law degree than it is for someone who left school at 16 with no GCSEs.

Under either regime the penalty could, in effect become zero – in cases, for instance, where there is nothing more serious than an honest mistake. However, whichever regime applies, the unpaid tax (and the appropriate interest on it) is always due in full. For serious cases, depending on the years involved, the old and new penalty rules may both apply until at least 2029.

In the 18th century Benjamin Franklin said that nothing is certain except death and taxes. In the 21st century the European Court of Human Rights established that death, in fact, is marginally more certain than taxes.

The Court ruled that penalties cannot be imposed on the living in respect of acts committed by a person or persons now deceased. Today nothing is certain except death and tax avoidance.

The termination

The ultimate aim of any negotiation with HMRC is to reach a settlement without a prosecution. This clears up the past and puts your affairs on the straight and narrow for the future.

The settlement is a contractual agreement involving a letter with a written offer to which there has to be a written acceptance. It also involves compromise, which is (by definition) something which leaves both sides less than perfectly content. If your advisers have done well, you will end up feeling less unhappy about the settlement than HMRC.

In order to collect unpaid tax, investigators have the right to seize your 'moveable' assets. For this they do not need to call on a bailiff. They just issue what is known as a 'walk-in possession order' and come and take goods to the value of the unpaid tax. However, they cannot as yet take money directly from your bank account without the permission of a court. Nor can they attempt to seize your home.

Because the proceeds from a sale of moveable assets are often not sufficient to cover penalties and unpaid tax

The ten golden rules for taxpayers who come under investigation by the SI

1 Keep calm and don't panic.

2 Get expert advice. It's always the cheaper option.

3 Don't discuss your tax affairs with anyone but a tight circle of professional advisers.

4 Don't lie to HMRC.

5 Don't assume that HMRC is ignorant of anything.

6 Be well prepared for meetings.

7 Make significant (but relevant) payments on account. HMRC sees this as an important sign of a willingness to cooperate.

8 Don't try to destroy evidence. It's usually unhelpful.

9 Do not suffer from selective amnesia when disclosing information involuntarily.

10 Once you've reached a settlement, don't offend again.

bills, HMRC has been trying to obtain the power to take money direct from bank accounts to meet unpaid tax bills. In a consultation paper on the subject it argued that taxpayers who owe money to HMRC 'frequently have sufficient funds or assets to pay their debts, but choose to delay doing so'. It cited the examples of Australia and France where it says tax authorities already have such powers.

Nevertheless, there are certain moveable assets that remain strictly out of bounds. These include the tools of your trade, the basic necessities of life, and perishable goods. Into the last category comes food, including frozen food. Hence, since frozen food cannot be taken, neither can a freezer. To a taxpayer looking at his otherwise decimated possessions, retaining a freezer might seem like cold comfort.

The only way an investigation can be brought to a formal end is by the issuance of a closure notice, a standard letter from HMRC declaring that it has closed the enquiry for good. After this, you cannot be quizzed about the same things again in respect of the same periods.

Most people who have been subjected to an investigation find that all their aches, pains and illnesses disappear, on average, within 30 seconds of reaching a settlement with HMRC. They may even feel inclined to kiss their mother-in-law and buy her another shawl.

Experience shows that termination also has a beneficial effect on other important aspects of life, such as:

- sleep;
- sex;
- bank managers;
- pets; and
- digestive systems.

AMEN

From start to finish –
a typical investigation

Notification letter from HMRC or voluntary disclosure
An investigation is prompted either when HMRC (see page 72) believes it has a case to pursue, or if you, the taxpayer, volunteer information to HMRC.

Appointment of advisers
When you are aware that an investigation is under way, appoint a team of professional advisers before you do anything else.

Initial meeting with HMRC
Your advisers will then meet HMRC in order to assess the seriousness of the case. At this stage it is not necessary for you to attend. In fact, it's better if you don't.

Code 9 or Code 8 investigation
You will then hear which of the two types of investigation your case comes under. Code 9 (or 'CIF', which stands for Civil Investigation of Fraud) means that you are under investigation for fraud. A Code 8 investigation involves other forms of non-payment.

Formal interview
This used to be known as the 'Hansard meeting', and it only takes place in a Code 9 investigation. It is based on five key questions (see page 88), and is attended by the CIF team, which may be local, or – if the amounts are large enough – part of the Specialist Investigations unit (SI), your advisers and you.

Scoping meeting
Later on, your advisers will meet the CIF team or SI unit again, this time to discuss the scope of the investigation.

↓

Preparation and submission of the report
Your adviser then prepares a report which represents your case to the CIF team or SI unit.

↓

Clarification meeting
The investigators may then wish to meet your advisers to discuss outstanding queries. This usually marks the beginning of the settlement negotiations.

↓

Settlement meeting
This marks the conclusion of the settlement negotiation. HMRC invites you to offer a settlement, which is usually a formality unless there are still issues to be resolved.

↓

Letter of offer
This is a formal letter to HMRC, prepared by your advisers and signed by you.

↓

Formal acceptance
HMRC replies in due course, confirming their acceptance of the offer.

Memorable lines

'The dog ate it'

Don't try to destroy evidence. You are quite likely to be found out and it will rebound against you. HMRC has recently obtained the same investigative powers as Customs & Excise. And these are considerable. It can in extreme cases bug phones and intercept e-mails and letters without any outside authorisation. One adviser says the new powers came as no surprise because he always knew 'there were a lot of buggers in HMRC'.

There are a number of excuses that HMRC will accept for lost documents or the late filing of a tax return, including:

- fire or flood in the post office where the documents were handled;
- prolonged industrial action by Post Office staff;
- loss through fire, flood or theft (but putting a cigarette lighter to last year's accounts does not work);

- very serious illness – such as a coma, a major heart attack, a stroke or any other serious mental or life-threatening condition (but note that the possibility of an HMRC enquiry is not in itself considered to be a life-threatening condition);
- the death of a close relative or (domestic) partner 'shortly before the deadline' – so don't think that granny's sad demise ten years ago will count.

There are also a number of excuses that HMRC has

made it clear it will not accept. Top of this list comes 'a shortage of funds'. Having no money is not considered a reasonable excuse for not paying tax. Other unacceptable excuses include:

- finding the forms too difficult to complete;
- the pressure of work;
- the shortcomings of a tax agent;
- a lack of information;
- the absence of any reminders from HMRC;
- being away on holiday.

By the way, removal vans very, very rarely lose accounting records. And it is almost equally rare for them to be destroyed in a flood. In one scene in the film, the main character is in a tax office claiming that a flood in the fifth-storey top-floor office of his accountant destroyed his records. (Note that, statistically, top-floor offices are about as likely to be flooded as the summit of Mount Ararat.) In the background the viewer can see that there is a pall of smoke rising from the surrounding buildings. The character in the film spots it and nervously asks the investigator what is going on. 'Don't worry,' replies the investigator, 'it's just another accountant's office being accidentally burned to the ground.'

'It's not fair'

Those who believe that a ruling by HMRC is not fair do have a right of appeal. Until April 2009, appeals were heard either by a body called the General Commissioners or by one called the Special Commissioners. Since April 2009 appeals have been heard by a Tribunal. There are two levels of Tribunal, a so-called 'first tier' and an 'upper tier'. After an appeal to the Tribunal, you still have a right to appeal directly to the courts.

There are some who argue that taxpayers are not treated as fairly as they used to be. In particular, they point to rules that were introduced in 2008 giving investigators new powers to seek out information. Investigators can now, for example, enter and inspect a business premises in order to look into a specific individual's tax affairs. And nobody, inside the business or outside, has a right to appeal against these 'raiders'. When the business premises are part of someone's home, then the raiders can be kept out of the domestic part of the building.

Developments such as this have nurtured demands for a formal Taxpayers' Charter, setting out your basic responsibilities and rights (including a statutory right to appeal). The government announced in April 2009 that a charter will be produced. But any charter must have teeth. In the movie you may just spot an illegible sheet of A4 paper stuck on the inside of an HMRC loo. Any delusions that such a document will suffice were 'flushed away' by the terms set out in the press release.

'How much is this gonna cost me?'

This question always tends to be asked too early in an investigation. Particularly by businessmen and entrepreneurs, people who are accustomed to knowing the full cost of everything before they will agree to buy anything.

There are three elements to the cost – the amount of previously unpaid tax that will have to be paid; the interest on that unpaid tax (which can be considerable if the investigation extends back over a number of years); and the penalties (see pages 89–92) that HMRC will impose for the incorrect returns that they have been provided with. None of these sums is going to be revealed with a great degree of accuracy until somewhere near the end of the movie. It is one of the main hooks keeping the audience in their seats until the very end.

'I'm going to complain about you to a higher authority'

If you feel you have reasonable grounds for a complaint, then HMRC has a standard procedure which makes it possible to appeal to more senior officials. Most complaints are sorted out at this level. There is also an 'impartial referee' called the Revenue Adjudicator, to whom complaints can be addressed. And you can, of course, always ask your MP to refer your case to the independent parliamentary ombudsman.

Some taxpayers are tempted to suggest that their human rights are being abused during an investigation. And European human rights legislation has occasionally been called upon in UK tax cases. But don't use these various complaints procedures for tactical purposes. Unless you have very sound reasons to complain, they are not going to help.

'Moi? Je suis propre'

Don't feign ignorance during an investigation, or pretend you don't understand English. And don't start talking to your adviser in a foreign tongue assuming you can't be understood. As their work has grown more international, so investigators have learned more foreign languages. There are now Russian speakers and Mandarin speakers among them, and several speak various Indian dialects. In any case, HMRC has never hesitated to call in interpreters.

Investigators are also skilled at understanding unspoken languages – the way letters are constructed, for instance, and the body language of people attending meetings. They can tell when someone has the weight of the world on their shoulders.

'Hypothetically speaking'

'Hypothetically' is a much-used (possibly over-used)

word in the *Taxman* movies. It means that what follows is exactly what has actually happened. As in: 'Hypothetically, I could have been putting all that into a Swiss bank account' or 'Hypothetically, I could have bought a yacht with that much money.'

Another favourite in the movie is 'serious consequences'. Tax investigators love to say things like: 'Serious consequences could follow from this.' When it was still known as the SCO, the SI was sometimes referred to as the Serious Consequences Office.

There are other phrases beloved by HMRC that are also not always what they seem. For example:

'We are disappointed with your report' probably means that
    HMRC has found a significant omission in it.
'Shouldn't you have another word with your client?' actually
    means: 'We really do have something on him.'
'This disclosure is not complete' could be a way of saying:
    'You've missed out a bank account or two.'
'Is there anything else you'd like to tell us?' means they are
    fishing.
'Can I come and see you again sometime soon?' to which the
    answer is yes, unless you want them to say: 'I'll
    serve a section 20 notice instead, and I might even
    raid your business premises too.'

'I won it on the dogs'

As a tactic, the gambling gambit rarely works. Casino records can be checked under the money-laundering legislation, and investigators know that any money bet on dogs is more likely to have gone to the dogs than anywhere else.

In general, it is best not to try and be funny with HMRC. (Most) investigators have a sense of humour, but they did not appreciate the taxpayer who filled in the box in a questionnaire that asked, 'Any other income?' with the words 'F All'. His seemingly inappropriate

Every tax investigator has a list of favourite excuses that he or she has heard taxpayers offer. Here are some of ours:

'Everybody does it … [pause] … don't they?'

'Do you call this a living?'

'I didn't gain from it personally.'

'I was ill, I had a nervous breakdown.'

'I always wanted to repay it.'

'I didn't think it was a lot of money – in those days.'

'I met this chap on a plane and he said it was all right.'

'I was ridiculed at the golf club because I didn't do it.'

'It's offshore, so I thought it would be okay.'

'Somebody advised me to do it. I can't remember who. He's dead now.'

'It was a gift.'

'I thought they'd never find it.'

'I had a handicapped child/sick relative that I was worried about.'

'It's not that serious … [long pause] … is it?'

'You think that's my only problem. I've got the Serious Fraud Office breathing down my neck as well.'

The special language of taxpayers

Just as tax investigators sometimes speak with a forked tongue, so too do taxpayers. Here are interpretations of some favourite phrases:

'I can't remember.' Advisers sometimes spend all day listening to their clients repeating: 'I can't remember.' They seem to forget how often they have already said it.

'Tell them they can go and rot in hell.' What this means is: 'I really want to settle urgently.'

'I only bought the yacht in order to charter it.' Meaning: 'I've already been round the world on it with my Russian girlfriend and a crew of six.'

'I don't care if this thing goes on for years.' This really means: 'If you don't settle within seven days I'm going to have a heart attack.'

'Do you remember everything that I tell you?' Or: 'I've said more than I wanted to.'

'Somebody told me that it happened to him.' This means: 'I'm telling you the truth now about what happened to me.'

'If I pay them £50,000, tell them to get off my back.' £50,000 seems to be the standard opening figure in any case where the final settlement should be in excess of £1 million.

'I'm totally innocent.' He or she is as guilty as hell.

language was only excused when he explained that he had meant it to stand for 'Family Allowance'.

'What! No discount? I got one last time'

HMRC does not like serial offenders. Penalties for a first offence are likely to be much smaller than those for repeat offenders. As the chairman of HMRC once put it: 'Why should we give taxpayers a second chance to have a good deal?'.

'Only little people pay taxes'

Ever since Leona Helmsley, an American heiress who owned a lot of hotels and almost as many small dogs, delivered this line to America's IRS, both the IRS and HMRC have been set on proving her wrong. In *Taxman* movies, the odds are stacked against the 'big people'. There's nothing that HMRC likes better than the publicity surrounding a famous person who gets caught up in a tax investigation – as in the cases, for instance, of Lester Piggott or Fabio Capello, England's football manager.

'Frankly, my dear, I don't give a damn'

The most famous last line in cinema history – Rhett Butler's words to Scarlett O'Hara, as delivered by Clark

Gable in *Gone With the Wind* – is a far cry from the last line in *The Taxman Always Rings Twice*. Tax investigators do very definitely give a damn, and they pursue cases to their bitter end. Nobody's slate is clean until 20 years have passed. And if payments under a settlement are not made on time the taxpayer very swiftly gets a call from HMRC's debt management unit. Its calls can, literally, continue beyond the grave.

Appendix:
'Direct' and 'indirect' taxes

In this book 'direct tax' includes:

- Capital gains tax
- Corporation tax
- Income tax
- Inheritance tax
- National Insurance contributions
- Petroleum revenue tax
- Stamp duty land tax
- Statutory payments
- Student loan repayments.

'Direct tax' also includes tax collected under Pay As You Earn (PAYE) and the Construction Industry Scheme.

In this book 'indirect tax' includes:

- Aggregates levy
- Air passenger duty

- Alcoholic liquor duties
- Amusement machine licence duty
- Bingo duty
- Climate change levy
- Counter-terrorism decisions
- Customs duty
- Gaming duty
- General betting duty
- Hydrocarbon oils duties
- Insurance premium tax
- Landfill tax
- Lottery duty
- Money laundering decisions
- Pool betting duty
- Remote gaming duty
- Tobacco products duty
- Value added tax (VAT).